DK EYEWITNESS WORKBOOKS

Insect

by Ben Hoare

Educational Consultants Linda B. Gambrell
and Geraldine Taylor

Senior Editors Susan Reuben, Fleur Star
Editor Anuroop Sanwalia
US Editor Jennette ElNaggar
Assistant Editor Lisa Stock
Art Editors Peter Laws, Tanisha Mandal
DK Picture Library Claire Bowers, Lucy Claxton,
Rose Horridge, Myriam Megharbi, Romaine Werblow
Managing Editors Christine Stroyan, Shikha Kulkarni
Managing Art Editors Anna Hall, Govind Mittal
DTP Designers Dheeraj Arora, Anita Yadav
Production Editor Tom Morse
Production Controller Rachel Ng
Senior Jacket Designer Suhita Dharamjit
Jacket Design Development Manager Sophia MTT
Publisher Andrew Macintyre
Art Director Karen Self
Publishing Director Jonathan Metcalf

This American Edition, 2020
First American Edition, 2008
Published in the United States by DK Publishing
1450 Broadway, Suite 801, New York, NY 10018

Copyright © 2008, 2020 Dorling Kindersley Limited
DK, a Division of Penguin Random House LLC
20 21 22 23 24 10 9 8 7 6 5 4 3 2 1
001–323002–Jun/2020

A catalog record for this book
is available from the Library of Congress.
ISBN 978-0-7440-3458-5

DK books are available at special discounts when purchased in bulk
for sales promotions, premiums, fund-raising, or educational use.
For details, contact: DK Publishing Special Markets,
1450 Broadway, Suite 801, New York, NY 10018
SpecialSales@dk.com

Printed and bound in Canada

For the curious
www.dk.com

Contents

Fast Facts

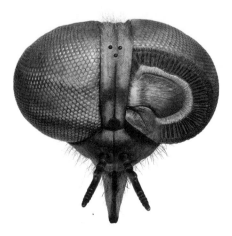

Activities

Quick Quiz

How This Book Can Help Your Child

Eyewitness Workbooks offer a fun and colorful range of stimulating titles in the subjects of history, science, and geography. Devised and written with the expert advice of educational consultants, each workbook aims to:

- develop a child's knowledge of a popular topic
- provide practice of key skills and reinforce classroom learning
- nurture a child's special interest in a subject.

About this book

Eyewitness Workbooks Insect is an activity-packed exploration of insects and their world. Inside you will find:

 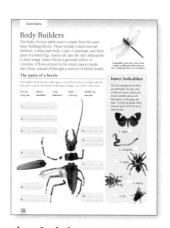 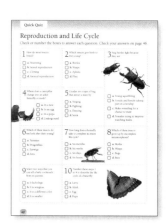

Fast Facts

This section presents key information as concise facts, which are easy to digest, learn, and remember. Encourage your child to start by reading through the valuable information in the Fast Facts section and studying the statistics chart at the back of the book before trying out the activities.

Activities

The enjoyable, fill-in activities are designed to develop information recall and help your child practice cross-referencing skills. Each activity can be completed using information provided on the page, in the Fast Facts section, or on the charts at the back of the book.

Quick Quiz

There are six pages of multiple-choice questions to test your child's newfound knowledge of the subject. Children should try answering the quiz questions only once all of the Activity section has been completed.

Important information

The butterfly bar activity on page 26 requires an adult to take part. Please also ensure that your child does not touch or pick up any insects he or she collects in the bug-hunting activity on page 37. All other activities in this book can be carried out without adult supervision.

PROGRESS CHART

Chart your progress as you work through the activity and quiz pages in this book. First check your answers, then color in a star in the correct box below.

Page	Topic	Star	Page	Topic	Star	Page	Topic	Star
14	Body Builders	☆	24	Social Insects	☆	34	Which Is Which?	☆
15	Staying in Touch	☆	25	Social Insects	☆	35	Which Is Which?	☆
16	Getting Around	☆	26	Butterflies and Moths	☆	36	The First Insects	☆
17	Hungry Mouths	☆	27	Flies	☆	37	Studying Insects	☆
18	Growing Up	☆	28	Beetles	☆	38	Body Parts and Classification	☆
19	Growing Up	☆	29	Bugs	☆	39	Habitats, Burrows, and Nests	☆
20	Insect Attack!	☆	30	Useful insects	☆	40	Reproduction and Life Cycle	☆
21	Insect Defenses	☆	31	Useful Insects	☆	41	Feeding and Defense	☆
22	Where Do They Live?	☆	32	Harmful Insects	☆	42	Insects on the Move	☆
23	Extreme Environments	☆	33	Insects under Threat	☆	43	Insects and People	☆

What Is an Insect?

The world is full of insects. They live all around us—on land, in water, in the air, and even underground. Insects come in many shapes and sizes. Many are quite small, but size is not the best way to tell whether an animal is an insect. There are several important features to look for, which you can read about on this page.

Parts of the body

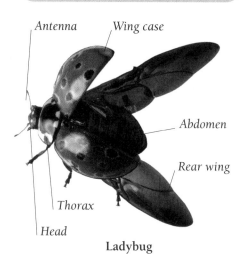

Ladybug

Adult insects always have three pairs of legs, and their body is divided into three parts—the head, thorax, and abdomen. On front of their head is a pair of feelers, called antennae. Young insects often look different from their parents, then change shape when they become adults.

Key facts

- The jaws of insects such as beetles are called mandibles.

- An insect's abdomen contains its heart, digestive system, and sexual organs.

- Insects don't have lungs. Instead, they breathe through tiny holes in their body, called spiracles. Each spiracle is connected to a tube that takes oxygen into the body.

Wings

Most adult insects have wings. Usually, they have four wings, but true flies have only two. Insect wings are thin and often transparent—you can see right through them. Beetles are different, because their front wings are thick and act as tough cases for their rear wings.

Key facts

- Insects were the first animals on Earth to have flapping wings.

- An insect's wings are fixed to its thorax, or middle body section, which also houses the powerful muscles it needs to fly.

- Insect wings are crisscrossed by a network of veins, which look like narrow lines. These carry blood and give the wings strength.

- When they are not flying, beetles fold their rear wings under their protective wing cases, which are often brightly colored.

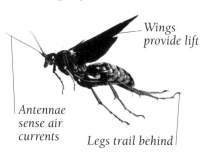

Wings provide lift

Antennae sense air currents

Legs trail behind

Spider wasp in flight

Legs and armor

Every insect is covered with a hard outer shell called an exoskeleton. This protects its entire body like a suit of armor. Insect legs are made up of four main parts, with a flexible joint between each section. The final section ends in a strong claw.

Exoskeleton

Golden beetle

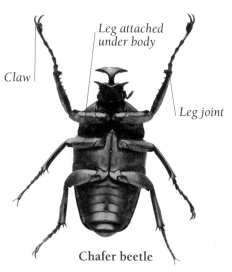

Leg attached under body

Claw

Leg joint

Chafer beetle

Key facts

- An insect's legs are joined to the underside of its thorax.

- Insect exoskeletons are made of chitin, the same tough substance from which crab shells are made.

- The surface of insect exoskeletons has a layer of wax on top. This makes insects waterproof so they don't lose water and dry out.

- As an insect grows up, it molts (sheds) its exoskeleton several times. Each time it does this, it grows a new, bigger exoskeleton.

The World of Insects

Insects make up more than half of all the animal species on the planet. There are probably millions of different kinds of insect, from tiny bugs smaller than a grain of sand to giant butterflies with wingspans the size of dinner plates. All insects are invertebrates, which means they do not have a backbone.

Meet the arthropods

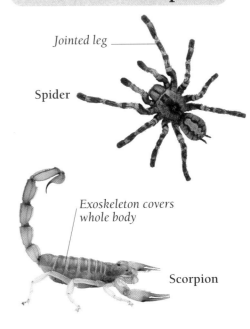

Jointed leg

Spider

Exoskeleton covers whole body

Scorpion

Wood louse

Insect groups

Each species of insects belongs to a larger group, or order, which contains other insects with similar physical features. For example, all the insects with one pair of wings are in the same group—the true flies. As well as a common name, every group has a scientific name in Latin.

Key facts

- Organizing species into groups is called classification.
- So far, scientists have identified more than a million species of insects. Many experts think there may be up to 10 million.
- Beetles form the largest order of insects. The next biggest insect order is butterflies and moths; then flies.

Common name	Scientific name	Number of species	
Ants, bees, and wasps	Hymenoptera	150,000	
Beetles	Coleoptera	400,000	
Butterflies and moths	Lepidoptera	180,000	
Flies	Diptera	160,000	
Bugs	Hemiptera	103,000	
Grasshoppers and crickets	Orthoptera	25,000	
Dragonflies and damselflies	Odonata	6,000	

An arthropod is any animal with jointed legs and an exoskeleton. Insects are arthropods, but not all arthropods are insects. Some other types of arthropods include spiders, wood lice, scorpions, centipedes, and millipedes. These creatures have a range of features that set them apart from insects.

Key facts

- Unlike insects, spiders and scorpions have eight legs and only two main body sections. They lack antennae and wings.
- Wood lice are distant relatives of crabs and lobsters, with a heavily armored shell. They are wingless and usually have 14 legs.
- Centipedes have long bodies with up to 300 legs. Millipedes have even more legs—sometimes as many as 750. That's 375 pairs!

Insect Senses

Insects have incredible senses that humans do not share, so we can only imagine what the world seems like to them. Most insects have several types of eyes, ears, and taste organs. They can smell tiny traces of chemicals and feel the smallest vibrations. Many can also see ultraviolet light and infrared radiation, which are invisible to us.

Sight

Most insects have a large pair of compound eyes. A compound eye has many lenses on its surface, which fit together like wall tiles. Each lens focuses light down through a tiny tube, which further fires information to the brain.

Cutaway model of a horsefly's eyes

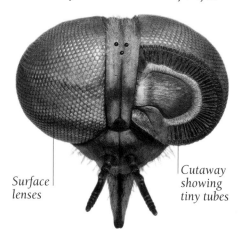

Surface lenses

Cutaway showing tiny tubes

Key facts

- Flies, dragonflies, and mantises have the largest insect eyes. Their eyes may cover their entire head!
- Many insects have three extra simple eyes, called ocelli, on top of their head. These detect light but do not create a full image.
- Insects see less detail than us but are very alert to movement. They react in an instant, which is why flies are so hard to swat.

Taste and smell

To an insect, tastes and smells are often more important than vision. As it goes about its life, the insect picks up thousands of chemical signals, which provide a nonstop flow of data to its brain. This information enables the insect to understand its surroundings, find food, and meet other insects.

Key facts

- Insect taste and smell organs are called chemoreceptors. They are located on the mouthparts, head, feet, and antennae.
- An insect's antennae are packed with tiny sensors that detect faint smells drifting in the air.
- Usually insects have long, mobile antennae to help them taste the air in every direction.
- Some bees, butterflies, and moths can smell a flower's perfume from 3 miles (5 km) away.

Flexible antenna made of many segments

Cockroach

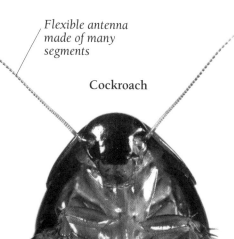

Touch and hearing

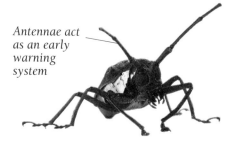

Antennae act as an early warning system

Longhorn beetle

Leg hairs

Body hairs

Bumblebee

Insects can feel and hear using virtually their whole body. This is because they are covered with sensitive hair, including on their legs and antennae and all over their head. The hair responds to touch, vibrations, and waves of sound moving through the air. In addition, most insects have several different ears, which may be on their abdomen, wings, or legs. Insects use sound to find and attract partners and to listen out for their enemies.

Key facts

- Insect antennae are never still—they twitch constantly to touch and investigate surfaces.
- Crickets have ears on their front legs. This is the ideal position as it allows them to feel vibrations in the ground.
- Insects can hear high-pitched sounds up to 200 kHz (kilohertz), which is well above the range of human hearing.

Insect Habitats

You can find insects almost anywhere on land, from hot deserts to snowy mountains. Some insects burrow in wood or soil, some live in caves or buildings, and many are found in fresh water. The ocean depths are the only habitat where insects cannot survive.

Plants

Habitats covered in lush green vegetation, such as forests and fields, have the most insects. Flowering plants and trees give insects somewhere to hide and provide them with a huge variety of food, including leaves, seeds, fruit, and nectar.

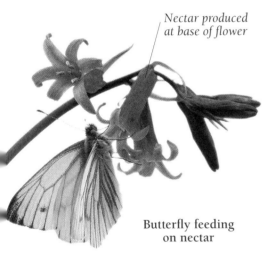

Nectar produced at base of flower

Butterfly feeding on nectar

Key facts

- Insects live on every part of plants—even the roots.
- Flowers are often buzzing with bees and butterflies, which visit to drink nectar. This sugary liquid contains lots of energy.
- In a forest, most insects live out of sight in the treetops or among fallen leaves on the ground.
- Grasslands are home to vast numbers of insects, especially ants, termites, and grasshoppers.

Fresh water

Lakes, ponds, marshes, rivers, and streams are full of insect life. Some insects never leave water, while others grow up there and then fly away to live in new areas. Insects have several different ways of surviving in water. They may swim to the surface to gulp air, or they may have a system for breathing underwater, like fish.

Key facts

- Diving beetles store bubbles of air under their wings so that they can breathe underwater.
- Young dragonflies, called nymphs, breathe by sucking water into their abdomen to extract oxygen. The adults are flying insects.
- Mosquitoes start life underwater and their larva (growing stage) has a breathing tube that it pokes above the surface like a snorkel.

Great diving beetle

Nests

Insects are skilled architects that make some very impressive nests for their eggs and young. A nest offers protection against predators and the weather. Some insects build a simple nest on their own. Other insects, such as ants, termites, and honeybees, build complex nest communities.

Hot air escapes at top

Hard earth walls

Termite nest

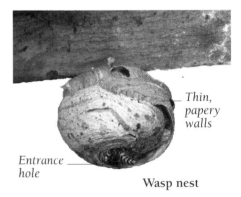

Thin, papery walls

Entrance hole

Wasp nest

Key facts

- The simplest nest is a burrow in the soil made by some wasps.
- Many termites make tower-shaped nests out of earth. The earth walls gradually bake hard in the sun.
- Termites control the temperature inside their nest by opening and closing ventilation holes.
- Wasp and bee nests usually have a single entrance hole to make them easier to guard against enemies.

Reproduction

Compared to many animals, most insects have short lives and breed very fast. Some breed when only a few hours old and die soon afterward. Insects breed by sexual reproduction—that is, males and females come together to mate. First, insects must find a partner, then they take part in courtship, and finally the female lays her eggs to produce a new generation of insects.

Mating

A pair of shield bugs mating

For many insects, mating lasts a matter of seconds, but bugs and dragonflies may stay joined for several hours. During mating, the male transfers sperm to the female, which she stores in her body to fertilize her eggs. The male plays no further part in producing young. A few female insects can breed by asexual reproduction—that is, without mating. Aphids, a type of tiny plant-eating bug, are able to breed in this way. The females produce babies even if they have never met a male aphid.

Sending signals

Insects have many ways of finding a partner. Some insects produce flashes of light or bursts of sound or perform a courtship dance. Female butterflies and moths release a perfume that is carried on the wind. Males follow the scent trail from far away to meet them.

Feathery antenna

Male moth

Key facts

- Male grasshoppers rub their long rear legs against their wings to make a buzzing courtship song.
- After dark, female fireflies signal to males with pulses of green light.
- Male moths often have large, feather-shaped antennae to help pick up the scent of females.
- Cicadas are bugs found in warm parts of the world. The males sing to attract females by vibrating a hard patch on their abdomen.

Fighting rivals

There is often competition for partners, with several males all trying to win a chance to mate. Many male beetles have large jaws to wrestle with their rivals. Stag beetles use their massive hornlike jaws to lift opponents off their feet and throw them onto the ground.

Key facts

- Before a fight starts, male stag beetles check out the size and strength of their opponent using their antennae.
- The losing stag beetle rarely dies, but he may be too injured to reproduce in future.
- Other male insects that fight for mates include dragonflies, some bees, and rhinoceros beetles.

Male stag beetles fighting

Huge jaws

Key facts

- Some male insects offer courtship gifts. Male dance flies perform a dance for the female and then give her a small fly to eat afterward.
- The female praying mantis seizes and eats her male partner after mating. This meal gives her extra energy to form the eggs.
- Adult mayflies live for between 30 minutes and 24 hours—just long enough to find a mate.

Life Cycles

Most insects begin life as eggs. Within a few days or weeks of being laid, each egg breaks open and a special growing stage, called a larva, crawls out. The larva may look nothing like its parents. The complex process by which the larva turns into an adult insect is known as metamorphosis. The word metamorphosis means to change body shape and appearance.

Changing shape

Many insects turn into adults by complete metamorphosis. The larva feeds and grows for a period of several weeks to a few years. Then it enters a resting stage called a pupa. During this stage, the larva's body is taken apart and reassembled into an adult insect.

Key facts

- Insects that develop by complete metamorphosis include beetles; butterflies and moths; flies; fleas; and ants, bees, and wasps.
- Usually the larva is wingless and the adult insect has wings.
- We often call butterfly and moth larvae "caterpillars," beetle larvae "grubs," and fly larvae "maggots."

Growing up

In grasshoppers and many other insects, the youngster changes into an adult gradually. It does not go through a dramatic change like a caterpillar when it becomes a pupa (see "Changing shape," left). Instead, the larva grows up steadily and replaces its exoskeleton regularly. Each time the larva grows a new exoskeleton, its body shape alters slightly. This process is known as incomplete metamorphosis.

Baby bugs cluster near their mother

Female shield bug guarding her brood

Key facts

- Insects that develop by incomplete metamorphosis include crickets and grasshoppers; dragonflies; termites; cockroaches; and bugs.
- The larvae of these insects are called nymphs. They often resemble miniature versions of their parents but lack wings.
- Aphids are bugs that don't lay eggs but give birth to live young.

Life cycle of a swallowtail butterfly

Egg attached to leaf stalk

Fat body with many small legs

1. Egg

2. Caterpillar

Pupa looks like dead leaf

Adult emerging from its pupa

Old pupal skin left behind

3. Pupa

4. Butterfly

Food and Feeding

Insects can eat almost anything, which is one reason why they are the most successful creatures on Earth. The many foods eaten by insects include plants, other insects, spiders, blood, decaying animal remains, paper, clothes, and even solid wood. Some insects eat only one or two foods, but others have a varied diet. The shape of an insect's mouthparts gives a clue to what it eats.

Suck and pierce

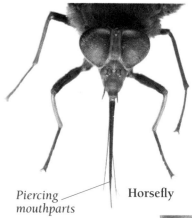

Piercing mouthparts   Horsefly

Chewing plants

Many insects have mandibles (jaws) adapted for chewing food. The mandibles have sharp cutting edges that quickly turn food into a sticky pulp ready for easy swallowing. Insects with chewing mandibles are mostly plant eaters, such as caterpillars, grasshoppers, crickets, and many beetle larvae.

Key facts

- Caterpillars are eating machines that munch leaves, starting from the outside of a leaf and working inward until it is stripped bare.
- Many caterpillars and beetle grubs nibble their way through crops and can be serious pests on farms.
- Plant-eating insects often have special bacteria in their gut that digest their food.

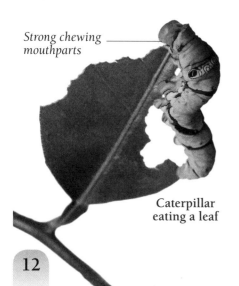

Strong chewing mouthparts

Caterpillar eating a leaf

Biting prey

Praying mantis eating a fly

Powerful front legs grip prey

Insect predators need to catch and chop up their prey so have the strongest jaws of all insects. Carnivorous (meat-eating) beetles have large, overlapping teeth on their jaws that work with a scissor action. They can kill animals larger than themselves, including caterpillars and fish.

Key facts

- Most insect predators eat using their jaws alone, but mantises seize prey in their front legs and hold the victims to devour them.
- Dragonfly larvae are ferocious predators, with hinged jaws that shoot forward like a harpoon to stab their prey before it escapes.

Aphids feeding on plant sap

Nymph

A large number of insects have jaws shaped like piercing needles, sponges, or long, sucking tubes. Mouthparts like these are suited to liquid foods such as nectar, blood, and sap—the sugary fluid inside plant stems. Houseflies eat leftovers and rotting meat, but before they can feed, they dissolve their meal by dribbling saliva over it. They use their spongelike mouthparts to mop up the resulting liquid.

Key facts

- Blood-sucking insects, such as horseflies and mosquitoes, have very fine, sharp mouthparts that can puncture skin.
- Butterflies and moths sip flower nectar using a long tongue called a proboscis. The proboscis coils up neatly when not in use.

How Insects Move

If insects were as big as humans, they would break all kinds of sporting records. They would run, leap, swim, and climb much faster and further than us. Insects weigh little, so accelerate quickly and are very maneuverable, and their six legs give them enough grip to hang upside down. Insects are masters of the air, too, and include some of the most acrobatic fliers in the animal world.

Fly

Insect wings are light but strong, which is the perfect combination for efficient flight. The powerful flight muscles beat the wings up and down thousands of times a minute, so they appear as a blur. Usually insects are superb fliers, apart from the heaviest beetles, which struggle to take off.

Key facts

- Dragonflies are the fastest fliers of all insects. Some reach speeds of 34 mph (55 km/h).
- Insect flight muscles work best when warm, which is why insects are more active on sunny days.
- Flies can flick their wings open in a split second, enabling them to take off almost right away.

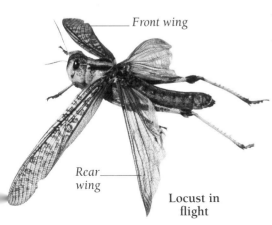

Front wing

Rear wing

Locust in flight

Swim

Water boatman

Moving in water is more difficult than moving in air. Water insects have developed several solutions to this problem. Many of them have broad, flattened legs that they use as paddles or oars. The water boatman rows along on its back and spends its entire life upside down. Pond skaters have a different strategy—these bugs have long, stiltlike legs to skim over the water surface.

Key facts

- Water beetles and bugs cannot walk on land. They travel to a new river, lake, or pond by flying.
- The legs of water insects have long fringes of hair to help propel them through the water.
- Mosquito larvae do not have legs and swim by wriggling their body from side to side in the water.

Burrow and jump

Many insects jump to escape their enemies, but for some, including grasshoppers, crickets, and fleas, leaping is the main form of movement. Some beetle larvae burrow inside dead trees and logs. They use their powerful jaws to excavate networks of tunnels through the soft wood.

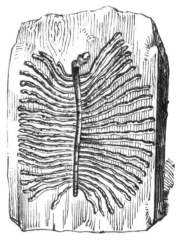

Beetle larva tunnels in wood

Flea

Long, strong back legs

Key facts

- Jumping insects, such as fleas, have large back legs to catapult them into the air. Fleas jump onto animals to suck their blood.
- A tiny flea can spring up to 12 in (30 cm) into the air—that's the same as a person jumping 25 ft (7.5 m) off the ground.
- Beetle larvae that bore into wood are often known as woodworms.

Body Builders

The body of every adult insect is made from the same basic building blocks. These include a hard external skeleton, a three-part body, a pair of antennae, and three pairs of jointed legs. Insects are also the only arthropods to have wings. Insect blood is greenish-yellow or colorless. It flows around in the empty spaces inside their body, instead of through a network of blood vessels.

Dragonflies can move their four wings in different directions at once, making them very aerobatic.

The parts of a beetle

This longhorn beetle has been taken apart to reveal the structure of its body. Label the body parts using the information on this page and page 6 as a guide. Choose from:

rear leg	thorax	wing	head	middle leg
wing case	mandible	abdomen	front leg	antenna

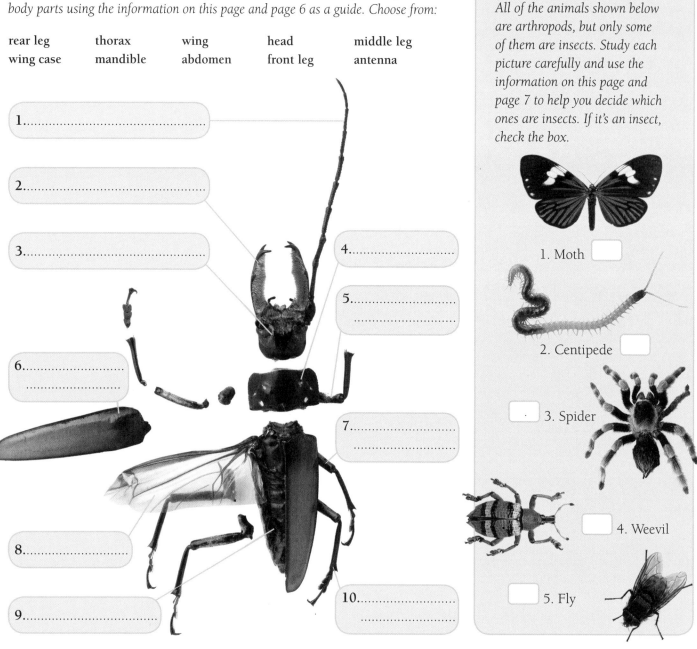

1.....................................

2.....................................

3.....................................

4.....................................

5.....................................
....

6.....................
....

7.....................................
....

8.....................................

9.....................................

10.....................................
....

Insect look-alikes

All of the animals shown below are arthropods, but only some of them are insects. Study each picture carefully and use the information on this page and page 7 to help you decide which ones are insects. If it's an insect, check the box.

1. Moth ☐

2. Centipede ☐

☐ 3. Spider

☐ 4. Weevil

☐ 5. Fly

Staying in Touch

Insects' sense organs are often very large compared to the rest of their body. If insects were as big as humans, some would have antennae as long as snooker cues and eyes the size of footballs. Their tiny brain can be smaller than the period at the end of this sentence, but it has enough power to process a constant flow of information about images, tastes, smells, vibrations, and sounds.

Wasp Alert!

Read the following explanation of how a wasp stays alert to its surroundings. Looking at the picture for clues, fill in the missing words. The information on page 8 will help you. Choose from:

compound eye   **antennae**   **lenses**   **hairs**   **simple eyes**

The common European wasp uses its pair of .... to detect smells in the air. On each side of its head is a massive .... extending from the jaws to the forehead. This complex structure is made up of thousands of tiny .... On top of the wasp's head, there are three ...., also known as ocelli, which cannot see things in detail but detect changes in the light. Almost the wasp's entire head is covered with sensitive .... that pick up even the smallest vibrations.

Feeling around

These pictures show some of the many types of insect antennae. Read each caption below, then write the letter of the picture it describes in the box.

1. When seen in close-up, the antennae of male moths look like feathers, with a central rod and dozens of small, hairy side branches.

2. Butterflies have thin antennae that end in a rounded club.

3. Bush locusts have long, wiry antennae that look like the ones on a radio.

4. Some beetles have enormous antler-shaped antennae that branch into many separate feelers.

5. Ants touch each other's antennae to pass on information, using different chemicals to send a variety of signals.

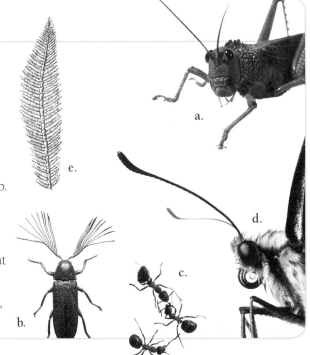

a.

e.

d.

c.

b.

Getting Around

Insects are superb athletes that are able to perform some breathtaking tricks. They can climb sheets of glass, fly backward, jump up to 40 times their own length, and fly across oceans. They can even keep moving after a predator has eaten their head, because they have several "mini-brains" that control different parts of their body.

Liftoff!

Draw lines from the captions to the different parts of this cockchafer beetle, which was photographed in midair shortly after takeoff. Use the information on page 6 to help you.

1. Wing cases open to give extra stability in the air

3. Antennae spread out to sense the air currents

4. Wings are made of a thin, transparent membrane

2. Beating wings provide the lift and driving force

5. Back legs trail behind to improve streamlining

Cockchafer in flight

Mix-and-match legs

These photographs show insects with different leg shapes. First read the descriptions, then match them to the pictures by writing the correct letter in each box.

a. The **green leaf insect's** front legs look like leaves to help it blend in with its surroundings.

b. A **cranefly** has thin, weak legs that may break off.

c. The **mole cricket** uses its long, strong claws for burrowing into the soil.

d. A **grasshopper** has powerful rear legs for jumping away from danger.

e. The **giant waterbug's smooth,** flattened legs work like paddles, enabling it to swim underwater.

1................... 2................... 3................... 4................... 5...................

Hungry Mouths

Scientists divide insects into four main groups according to their diet. Plant eaters feed on every part of plants. Predators kill and eat a wide range of small creatures. Scavengers eat dead animal remains and rotting plant matter. The final group of insects—insect parasites—are a special case. They live on or inside another animal, known as their host, and feast on the host's body.

Did you know?

Scavengers like this cockroach play a vital role in the natural world by cleaning away all kinds of remains and leftover food.

Different diets quiz

Circle the correct words to complete these statements about different insect diets. Use the information on this page and page 12 to help you.

1. Caterpillars have powerful **sucking / chewing** mouthparts for eating leaves.

2. Mantises are fast-moving **predators / scavengers** of other insects and spiders.

3. Horseflies use their **club-shaped / needlelike** mouthparts to feed on blood.

4. Cockroaches eat mainly waste food and **living animals / dead animals**.

5. Blood-sucking fleas are **parasites / scavengers** found in the fur of mammals such as cats, dogs, and rabbits.

6. Aphids are tiny **flesh-eating / plant-sucking** bugs.

Food web puzzle

A food web is a diagram that uses arrows to show what eats what in a particular habitat, such as a forest or pond. Read the statements below about the animals and plants in this garden food web. Then write the correct letter in each box to match the descriptions up with the pictures.

 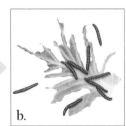   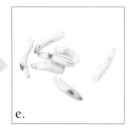

a.   b.   c.   d.   e.

1. Ground beetles prey on other insects, especially juicy caterpillars.

3. Caterpillars have huge appetites and can soon strip entire plants bare.

5. Vegetables are a favorite food for plant-eating insects and their larvae.

2. Many garden birds feed on beetles.

4. When a bird dies, its body is eaten by scavengers such as maggots (fly larvae).

Growing Up

Insects that develop by complete metamorphosis have very different lives as young and adults. Often the larvae specialize in eating and the adults specialize in breeding. Most insects that grow up by incomplete metamorphosis lead similar lives when nymphs and adults.

Young insects puzzle

Each of these pictures shows a young insect, or nymph, that turns into an adult by incomplete metamorphosis. Read the captions, then write the name of the correct nymph under each picture.

- A **bug nymph** looks like a miniature copy of its parents. The young of some bugs cluster together for defense.

- A **damselfly nymph** lives in ponds and streams. It uses fan-shaped structures called gills on the end of its abdomen to breathe oxygen underwater.

- A **froghopper nymph** produces foam like bubble bath to stop itself from drying out and give protection from enemies. This has earned it the nickname of "spit bug."

- A **cockroach nymph** has a shiny brown body similar to an adult, but it is smaller and lacks wings.

1...

2...

3...

4...

Insect metamorphosis

Complete this table to show how different insects grow up. Check the correct boxes to indicate whether each type of insect develops into an adult by complete or incomplete metamorphosis. Use the information on page 11 to help you.

Insect group	Complete metamorphosis	Incomplete metamorphosis
Beetles		
Grasshoppers and crickets		
Butterflies and moths		
Dragonflies and damselflies		
Flies		
Ants, bees, and wasps		
Bugs		
Cockroaches		

Development of a red admiral butterfly

Read these descriptions of how a red admiral butterfly develops from an egg into a winged adult. Then draw the missing pictures from the butterfly's life cycle. Use the pictures on page 11 to help you.

Egg

The red admiral butterfly begins life as a tiny egg, which is green to camouflage it from hungry birds. The egg is fastened to a leaf, and after about a week it hatches into a wriggling caterpillar.

Caterpillar

Like many caterpillars, the red admiral caterpillar eats only one type of plant. It munches stinging nettles but does not suffer the burning sensation we do if we touch the plant's leaves.

Pupa

When it has finished growing, the caterpillar clings to a stinging nettle stem and turns into a pupa. The outside of the pupa becomes a tough case. Safe inside, the caterpillar changes into a butterfly.

Hatching

As the pupa develops, the bright colors of the growing butterfly start to show through the case. When the pupa is about 10 days old, it splits open and the adult butterfly struggles free.

Butterfly

At first, the freshly emerged butterfly has weak, floppy wings. It stays still while blood pumps into the wings to harden them. Finally, it takes off to search for flowers to drink the nectar.

Insect Attack!

Insects have an impressive range of weaponry. Beetles, dragonflies, and mantises use their powerful mouthparts to give a lethal crunching bite. Predatory bugs suck the life out of their prey. Wasps are equipped with painful stings, and assassin bugs inject poison into their victims. Ants use strength in numbers and attack in groups.

Did you know?

The larva of the antlion makes a trap to catch prey. It digs a funnel-shaped hole in sand and lies hidden at the bottom, waiting for ants to tumble in.

Insect predator quiz

Use the information on this page and on the charts at the back of the book to help you answer these questions about insect predators.

1. Which bug uses its long, sharp beak to stab its prey and inject it with poisonous saliva? ....

2. Which beetle larva is one of the most aggressive predators found in garden ponds? ....

3. Which part of the body does the praying mantis use to snatch its prey? ....

4. Do wood ants hunt for food alone or in groups? ....

5. How does the weevil wasp manage to kill prey larger than itself? ....

6. Which colorful garden beetle eats aphids? ....

Great diving beetle larva catching a small fish

Wasp sting

Read the following explanation of how a wasp stings its prey with venom (poison). Looking at the cutaway diagram for clues, fill in the missing words. Choose from:

venom sac   barb   muscular pouch   abdomen

A wasp's sting is at the end of its ....

When the wasp seizes its prey, the sting slides out into

position. The sharp .... at the tip pierces

the body of the victim. Venom is stored in the wasp's

.... A powerful ....

pumps the venom through the sting into the prey.

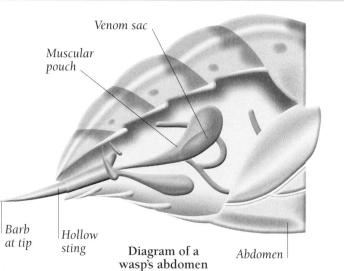

Venom sac

Muscular pouch

Barb at tip

Hollow sting

Diagram of a wasp's abdomen

Abdomen

Insect Defenses

Life is dangerous for insects because many animals eat them. To avoid their predators, insects have an amazing variety of defenses. Some use speed to escape, some use camouflage, and some are poisonous or dangerous to handle. Others trick or confuse their enemies to escape.

Hide and seek puzzle

Look closely at these camouflaged insects, then draw a line from each insect to the habitat in which it is best hidden.

1.

Indian leaf butterfly

a.

2.

Rainforest grasshopper

b.

3.

Thorn bug

c.

4.

Peppered moth

d.

5.

Stick insect

e.

Avoiding predators

Read these descriptions of insect defenses. Then match the correct image to each caption.

1. The **caterpillar of the postman butterfly** is protected by a long line of poisonous spikes down its back.

a.
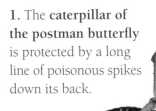

2. The **pine emperor moth** has big, staring "eyes" that appear dangerous and deter predators.

b.

3. Bombardier beetles squirt a powerful jet of hot chemicals from the tip of the abdomen to drive away attackers.

c.

4. This **hoverfly** is harmless, but because it looks like a wasp, predators are tricked into leaving it alone.

d.

5. The **New Zealand weta** waves its back legs around in the air to make itself look larger and more frightening.

e.

Where Do They Live?

Insects live virtually all over the world, but they are not spread evenly. They prefer warm climates, so there are few insects at the poles. The closer to the Equator you go, the more insects there are. Tropical rain forests have more insects than anywhere else on Earth.

Insect habitats

Read these descriptions of different insects and the habitats in which they live. Then fill in the missing words. Choose from:

bumblebees   cave crickets   desert beetles   dragonflies   dung beetles   giant Atlas moth

Rain forest

The .... lives in rain forests in Southeast Asia. It is the world's largest moth, with a wingspan of up to 12 in (30 cm).

Cave

Unlike crickets that live above ground, ... are sightless. They use their extra-long antennae to feel their way in the dark.

Grassland

.... live where there are herds of grazing animals and roll away balls of dung to use as food for their larvae.

Desert

Many .... do not need to drink and feed at night to avoid the scorching daytime heat.

Stream

.... lay their eggs in fresh water. Their larvae live underwater, then crawl out to turn into adults.

Garden

Flowers attract ...., which drink the sugary nectar and eat some of the pollen as well.

Extreme Environments

Many insects can cope with very harsh conditions. Their outer skeleton gives protection against the hot and cold, keeps out the wind and rain, and prevents them from drying out. During bad weather, insects save energy by becoming less active, but when conditions get tough, they stop moving altogether and enter a resting state.

True or false?

Read the following sentences about insect survival. Using the information in the facts box to help you, check the boxes to show which facts are true and which are false.

	TRUE	FALSE
1. In cold climates, insects stay alive because a chemical stops their blood from freezing.	☐	☐
2. When an insect hibernates, all of its body processes speed up.	☐	☐
3. Muddy ponds have too little oxygen for anything to live there.	☐	☐
4. Ants can keep moving even in extremely hot conditions.	☐	☐
5. High mountains are empty of insect life.	☐	☐

Survival strategies

Circle the correct words to complete each sentence below. Use the information on this page and page 9 to help you.

1. Insects survive droughts because their **internal / external** skeleton means they don't dry out.

2. Termites are able to control the **temperature / light level** inside their nests made of sun-dried earth.

3. Diving beetles can live underwater because they store a supply of **air / food** under their wings.

4. On cold and wet days, honeybees save valuable energy by becoming **more / less** active and staying in their nest.

5. Wasp nests have **a single entrance hole / several entrance holes** to make the nest easier to defend.

Did you know?

Some flies live on floating mats of vegetation next to bubbling hot springs, where temperatures may reach 109°F (43°C).

Insect survival facts

Arctic landscape

- In an experiment, ants remained active when heated to 150°F (65°C). Humans would pass out!

- Some fly larvae can thrive in murky ponds where there is almost no oxygen.

- Insects in the Arctic and Antarctic have an antifreeze called glycerol in their blood. This chemical protects them against the extreme cold.

- Stoneflies and bees have been seen on mountains at heights over 18,000 ft (5,500 m).

- Resting insects fall into a deep sleep called hibernation, in which they shut down their body functions.

Social Insects

Social insects live together in a family group called a colony and work as a team to build a nest. The insects in the colony are split into several different castes (types) that each carry out different tasks. All ants and termites are social insects, and many bees and wasps are, too.

Living together facts

- A single female—the queen—lays all of the colony's eggs.
- Most of the colony are workers. They look after the queen's eggs and larvae, gather food, and repair the nest.
- In honeybee nests, the workers are always female.
- Male honeybees, or drones, fly in search of queens to mate with to start new nests.
- Some ant colonies contain soldier ants, which fight off predators.

Honeybee workers with their queen

True or false?

Read the following sentences about social insects. Using the information on this page, check the boxes to show which facts are true and which are false.

	TRUE	FALSE
1. The main task of insect workers is to lay eggs.	☐	☐
2. Ants and termites always live in groups.	☐	☐
3. Soldier ants help protect the rest of the ants living in the same nest.	☐	☐
4. Worker honeybees are usually male.	☐	☐
5. The name for a group of social insects is a colony.	☐	☐

Termite city

Each termite colony builds a moundlike nest, which may be home to up to 5 million termites. Read these descriptions of the features of a termite mound, then fill in the missing labels on the picture.

- Large **royal cell** near the base of the mound houses the egg-producing queen termite.
- Thick **clay wall** gives protection against predators.
- Waste hot air escapes through main **ventilation chimney**.
- **Side vents** bring fresh air into the nest.
- Eggs and larvae are kept in a network of **nursery chambers**.

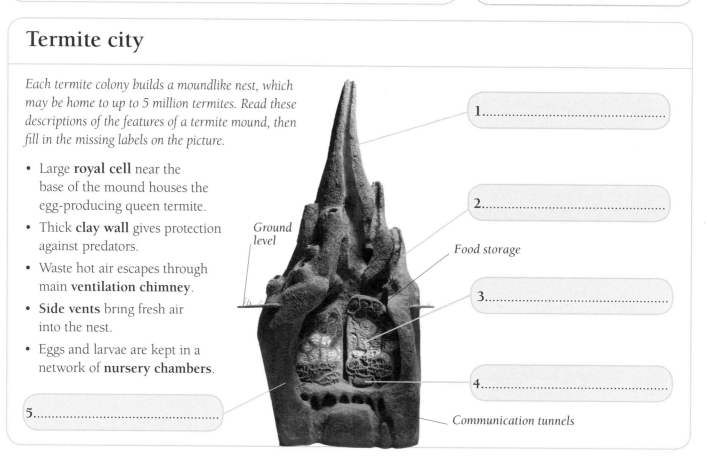

Ground level

1. ....

2. ....

Food storage

3. ....

4. ....

Communication tunnels

5. ....

Building a nest

The nests made by common wasps are started in spring by a queen wasp. Later in the year, the newly hatched worker wasps help her. Look at the photographs, which show how the nest takes shape. Then read the captions below and number them 1 to 6 in the right order.

1.

a. The queen extends the nest, and her eggs begin to hatch into fat, gray wasp larvae, which develop inside their separate cells.

b. By the summer's end, the nest is a large ball of many spiral layers and is buzzing with lots of wasps.

c. Now the queen lines the nest with small pockets called cells, then lays one egg at the bottom of each cell.

2.    3.    4.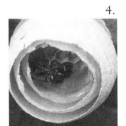

d. In spring, the queen wasp wakes up hungry, having slept all winter. She goes on a hunting trip to boost her low energy levels.

e. When the larvae hatch into new wasps, these workers add more layers of "paper" to the rapidly expanding nest.

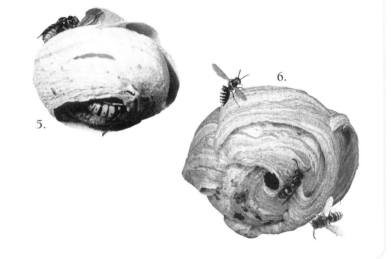

5.   6.

f. The queen starts to build the walls of her nest by chewing pieces of wood and mixing it with her saliva to make a paperlike material.

Together or alone?

Complete this table by checking the right boxes to indicate whether each insect lives together in groups or lives mainly on its own. Use the information on the page opposite to help you. (Hint: only the insects listed opposite are social insects.)

Insect	Lives together	Lives alone
Ant		
Grasshopper		
Honeybee		
Termite		
Mantis		

Butterflies and Moths

Butterflies and moths have two pairs of broad wings covered in thousands of tiny scales. As adults, they feed on liquids such as flower nectar, which they suck up using their long, tube-shaped proboscis (tongue).

Identification facts

- Some male butterflies have scent scales on the rear wings, which scatter perfume to attract females.

Agrias butterfly

- All butterflies fly during the day. Moths usually fly at night, although a few are active in broad daylight.

- Many butterflies have colorful wings. Some moths are brightly patterned, too, but most are gray or brown.

- Butterflies have long, thin antennae that end in a rounded club. Moths have thicker antennae, which may be straight or feathery.

- Unless they are sunbathing, butterflies usually rest with their wings folded upright over their bodies. Most moths lay their wings flat.

Identification puzzle

Read the following description of the differences between butterflies and moths. Then fill in the missing words, using the information on this page to help you. Choose from:

**after dark   flat   eye-catching   during the day   dull and drab
folded   thicker**

Butterflies are some of the most .... insects, whereas

moths tend to be .... You can see moths at night or

.... , but butterflies never fly ....

Moths have .... antennae compared to butterflies. One of

the best ways to tell butterflies and moths apart is to look at their wings

when they land. A butterfly normally rests with its wings .... ,

while a moth is more likely to keep its wings ....

Make a butterfly bar

! Ask an adult to heat the mixture in step 2.

To get a good look at butterflies feeding, you can make a butterfly bar. The bar serves a sticky mixture of sugar and sweet fruit—the perfect energy food for hungry butterflies.

Ask an adult to help you heat the fruit mixture! Remember that butterflies are more active in warm, sunny weather, so choose a nice summer day to open your bar.

1 Peel an overripe banana, slice it into a bowl, and mash it up with a fork.

2 Mix the mashed banana with sugar and water, then ask an adult to help you heat the paste gently in a pan until it becomes brown and sticky. Let it cool.

3 Make three evenly spaced holes near the rim of a paper plate. Thread a piece of string through all of the holes and tie it at the top to make a hanging loop.

4 Smear some of the banana paste onto the plate. Now hang your finished butterfly bar outside where you can see it.

How many butterflies did you see feeding each day? ....

How many different kinds of butterflies did you attract? ....

Did any other insects visit your bar? If so, which ones? ....

Flies

Flies are extremely acrobatic insects that can fly backward, hover, and even walk upside down. Unlike most other flying insects, they have only one pair of wings. There are thousands of different flies, including houseflies, midges, gnats, and mosquitoes.

Life cycle facts

- The female bluebottle fly lays her eggs on a dead animal.
- Each egg hatches into a legless maggot within 24 hours.
- The maggot feeds nonstop and grows rapidly. It turns into a pupa 10 days later.
- Inside the pupa, the maggot's body changes into an adult fly. The fly emerges after 12 days.
- The adult fly is able to breed a day after hatching and lives for two to three weeks.
- The bluebottle's total life span, from egg to adult, is six weeks.

Bluebottle life span

Many flies are very short-lived and can complete their entire life cycle, from egg to adult, in only a few weeks. Read the facts box about the life cycle of the bluebottle fly (left). Then fill in the timeline below by writing how long the bluebottle usually spends at each stage of its life.

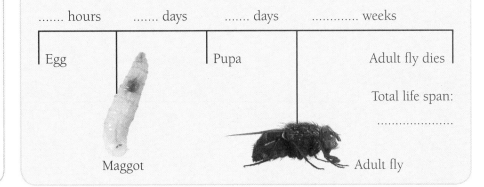

.... hours   .... days   .... days   .... weeks

Egg   Pupa   Adult fly dies

Total life span: ....

Maggot   Adult fly

Population explosion

Flies breed so fast that if conditions are good, they can increase in numbers amazingly quickly. Read the example below, which shows how a fly population grows over three generations. Then figure out how many flies there could be in the third generation. Use a calculator to help you.

Generation 1 (weeks 1–6)
The two parent flies produce 200 young (100 males and 100 females). The new generation has 100 breeding couples.

Generation 2 (weeks 7–12)
The 100 breeding couples also produce 200 young each. This gives a total of 20,000 flies (100 x 200), and so there are now 10,000 breeding couples.

Generation 3 (weeks 13–18)
The 10,000 breeding couples all produce 200 young. How many flies might there be now?

....

Check your answer on page 45.

Mopping up

Circle the correct words to complete each sentence below. Use the information on page 12 to help you.

1. A housefly can feed only on **liquid / solid** food.
2. Before it starts to eat, the fly dribbles **poison / saliva** over everything.
3. This helps **dissolve the food / kill its prey**.
4. Now the fly uses its **chewing / spongelike** mouthparts to hoover up its meal.

Beetles

Beetles are more varied in size, shape, and behavior than any other group of insects. The smallest beetles are only the size of a pinhead and the largest weigh five times more than a house mouse. Every beetle has body armor made from its extra-tough front wings, which slide over the back wings to protect them.

Fighting beetles

Circle the correct words to complete each sentence, using the information on page 10 to help you.

1. Male stag beetles fight each other for **food / females**.

2. They are named for their **claws / jaws** like horns.

3. Before fighting, rivals use their **antennae / front legs** to size each other up.

4. As the fight begins, each beetle tries to **bite / lift up** its opponent.

5. The **winner / loser** ends up on the ground.

Beetling about

Look at these beetles and beetle larvae, then draw a line to match each one with its favorite food. Use the information on this page and on the back cover chart to help you.

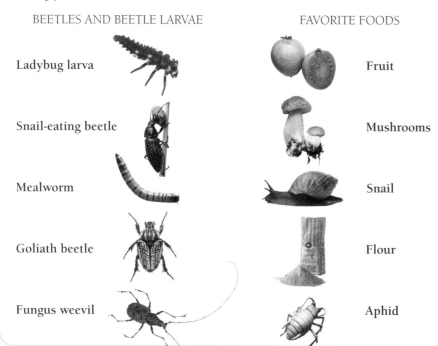

BEETLES AND BEETLE LARVAE   FAVORITE FOODS

Ladybug larva   Fruit

Snail-eating beetle   Mushrooms

Mealworm   Snail

Goliath beetle   Flour

Fungus weevil   Aphid

Did you know?

The giraffe beetle uses its amazingly long, cranelike neck to roll up leaves into a snug nest. It lives in rain forests on Madagascar, off the coast of East Africa.

Giraffe beetle

Beetle diet facts

- Beetles eat a huge variety of foods, from living prey to dead animals, crops, dung, rotting vegetation, kitchen scraps, and even clothing.

- Longhorn beetles eat wood during their larval stage, helped by microorganisms in their gut that digest wood.

- Mushrooms are food for several beetles, including fungus weevils.

- Some beetles are a serious nuisance. Mealworm beetle larvae, called mealworms, feast on stored grain and flour in warehouses and cellars.

- Some beetles are helpful. Ladybugs and their larvae are fierce predators of aphids and other insect pests.

A pair of ladybugs

Bugs

The word "bug" is often used for any small creature with legs, but bugs are actually a separate group of insects. Bugs have two pairs of wings, and their mouthparts are adapted as a long feeding tube for sucking and piercing. Many bugs use the tube to lap up plant sap, and others drink blood or suck the juices of their prey.

Walking on water

Pond skaters live in freshwater habitats and skim across the surface of water without sinking. To find out how they walk on water, try this simple experiment.

A pond skater glides over water to catch its prey.

1 Fill a large glass or bowl with water. Wait until the surface is completely still.

2 Now pick up a paper clip using a pair of tweezers and carefully lower it onto the water.

3 Does the paper clip float or sink? Can you think why? Turn to page 45 to see why this happens.

Mealtime

Check the correct box to show which bugs are predators and which are vegetarian. Use the information on this page to help you.

	Predator	Vegetarian
1. Planthopper	☐	☐
2. Pond skater	☐	☐
3. Assassin bug	☐	☐
4. Mealy bug	☐	☐
5. Sea skater	☐	☐

True or false?

Read the following sentences about bugs. Using the information on this page to help you, check the boxes to show which facts are true and which are false.

	TRUE	FALSE
1. All bugs are harmless to people.	☐	☐
2. The mouthparts of bugs are a long and hollow tube like a drinking straw.	☐	☐
3. Mealy bugs are the biggest type of bug.	☐	☐
4. Cicadas have the loudest calls of any bug.	☐	☐
5. Bugs have four wings.	☐	☐

Bug facts

- Bugs go through incomplete metamorphosis and the young look like tiny versions of their parents (see page 11).

- The largest bugs are giant water bugs up to 6 in (15 cm) long.

- Male cicadas are the world's noisiest insects. Their buzzing courtship songs can be as loud as a power saw.

- Small sap-sucking bugs such as aphids, planthoppers, and mealy bugs are major pests of crops and gardens.

- In South America, blood-sucking assassin bugs spread Chagas disease, which can be fatal in humans.

Useful Insects

Many insects are useful—in fact, we could not survive without them. Insects help pollinate crops and give us products such as honey and silk. Some control the pests that attack our plants and food, and others are scavengers that clear away waste and dead bodies.

Nature's helpers

Read the introduction and facts box (right) on this page, then complete these statements about the ways insects can be helpful. Choose from:

spin   crush   scavenge   control   pollinate

1. Carrion beetles help control disease because they .... the bodies of dead animals.

2. Many bees, butterflies, and moths help .... crops.

3. Silkworms .... a material we use to make clothing.

4. Predatory insects help .... pests such as slugs and snails.

5. We .... dead scale insects to make food coloring.

Made by insects

None of the things illustrated here could exist without insects. Write the name of the insect that helped produce each item, using the information in the facts box to help you.

Product: Silk scarf

Insect: ....

Product: Candle

Insect: ....

Product: Red food coloring

Insect: ....

Product: Honey

Insect: ....

Did you know?

Carrion beetles help prevent disease, because they scavenge the bodies of animals when they die.

Insect product facts

- Silk is a luxurious fiber spun by silkworms—the caterpillars of silk moths.

Bee hives

- Honeybees produce honey from nectar and feed it to their larvae. We get most of our honey from bees kept in hives and the rest comes from wild bee nests.

- Worker honeybees also produce wax to build cells for their larvae to grow in. The beeswax can be turned into sweet-scented candles.

- Bees, butterflies, and moths are important on farms and in gardens, because they help pollinate crops and other useful plants.

- A red food coloring called cochineal is made by crushing the bodies of scale insects. These tiny bugs are raised on special farms in Mexico ready for harvesting.

Pollination puzzle

Look carefully at these pictures of a bumblebee pollinating a flower. Then read the labels below and fill in the missing words, using the information on this page to help you. Choose from:

hairy body   petals   proboscis   stamens   antennae

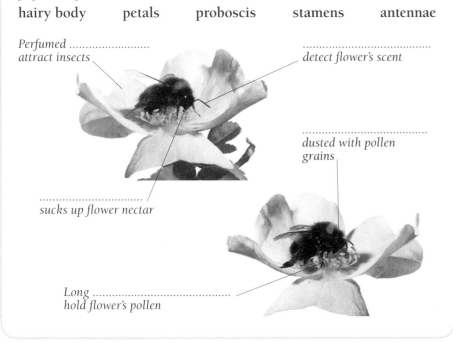

Perfumed ....
attract insects

....
detect flower's scent

....
dusted with pollen
grains

....
sucks up flower nectar

Long ....
hold flower's pollen

Cleaning up

Dung beetles play an important part in the natural world by recycling animal droppings as food for their grubs. Look at the pictures below showing a dung beetle at work, then circle the correct words to complete each sentence.

The beetle gathers bits of cattle dung and pats them into a **tube / ball**. This is usually **larger / smaller** than the beetle itself. It uses its strong **legs / wings** to push the dung along the ground.

Next, the beetle digs a **tunnel / mound** as a nest. It fills the nest with plenty of dung for its **grubs / mate** to eat. Finally, the beetle lays its eggs and seals the entrance to the nest.

Pollination facts

- Flowers reproduce by exchanging pollen, which enables them to make seeds. This is called pollination.

- Pollen is a dustlike material that contains a plant's male sex cells.

- Insects such as bees, butterflies, and moths carry pollen from flower to flower. Many flowers have scented petals to attract these pollinators.

**Pollen grain
(magnified)**

- An insect picks up a flower's perfume using its antennae. It follows the scent trail, and when it lands, it brushes against the flower's stalklike stamens (the male parts). These dust its body with pollen.

- If the insect visits another flower, the pollen already on its body rubs off onto the flower's stigmas (the female parts) to pollinate the plant.

- In return for carrying pollen for the plant, insects get a reward of nectar, which they sip using their long proboscis.

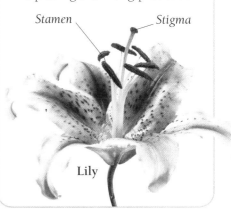

Stamen   *Stigma*

Lily

Harmful Insects

Many insects are pests because they damage our plants, buildings, food stores, and clothes. Each year, they ruin about 15 percent of the world's crops. Insects can also give painful bites or stings. When blood-sucking flies, fleas, and bugs bite people, they can spread disease.

Malaria facts

- Malaria is a disease caused by a microscopic parasite that lives inside mosquitoes in hot, tropical countries.

- When an infected mosquito bites someone, the malaria parasite enters the person's bloodstream.

Mosquito

- The parasite invades the person's liver cells, where it starts to multiply.

- As the parasite multiplies, the victim suffers severe fever and sometimes kidney damage, which can be fatal.

- Each year, malaria infects 200 million people and kills about half a million of them, mainly in tropical parts of Africa.

True or false?

Read the following sentences about malaria. Using the information in the facts box (right), check the boxes to show which facts are true and which are false.

	TRUE	FALSE
1. People catch malaria when a mosquito carrying the parasite bites them.	☐	☐
2. Everyone infected with malaria dies from it.	☐	☐
3. Malaria is a health hazard mostly in warm climates in the tropics.	☐	☐
4. The usual symptom of malaria is a high fever.	☐	☐
5. Malaria parasites start to multiply in the stomach.	☐	☐

Insect damage

Look at these pictures of the damage caused by insects. Then write the name of the insect responsible. Choose from:

Larder beetle   **Woodworm**   **Clothes moth**   **Caterpillar**

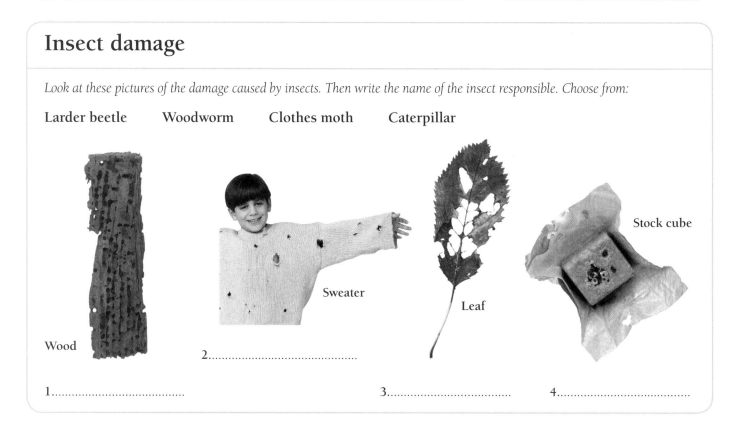

Stock cube

Sweater

Leaf

Wood

1................................

2................................

3................................

4................................

Insects under Threat

More and more insects are threatened. They are at risk from the destruction of forests, grassland, and wetlands, and from the conversion of land to farming. Chemical pesticides kill huge numbers of insects, including harmless species as well as pests. This improves harvests, but it disrupts the world's natural environment.

Insect threat facts

- Modern buildings have fewer cracks and crevices for wasps and ants to make their nests.
- Dragonflies are threatened by the drainage of pools and marshes.
- Weed killers wipe out the wildflowers that many bees rely on for food.
- In rain forests, colorful beetles and butterflies are captured and mounted for sale as tourist trinkets.
- Many beetles are affected when dead trees are cleared from forests—the developing beetle larvae need rotting wood to eat while they grow.

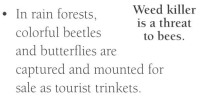

Weed killer is a threat to bees.

Insect threat test

Read the facts box (right) that explains some of the dangers facing insects today. Then complete these sentences by writing the name of the insects at risk.

1. The removal of decaying trees harms populations of ....
2. Many new buildings have nowhere for .... and .... to live.
3. Some tropical .... and .... are endangered because they are sold as souvenirs.
4. Draining wetlands puts .... in danger.
5. .... are threatened by the use of weed killers.

Create an insect refuge

Gardens can be great places for insects, so why not create your own nature reserve? Read these tips that explain how to make even a small garden into a haven for all kinds of insects. Then number the boxes to match each tip to the right picture.

1. Don't burn leaves—leave them in a heap in a quiet corner. It will provide a safe hiding place for beetles, bugs, and earwigs.
2. Avoid spraying flower beds with pesticides. Let them grow wild, and insect predators will arrive to do the job for you.
3. Plant sweet-scented flowers to attract bees, moths, and butterflies. A good choice is lavender, which is easy to grow and has lovely purple flowers on long stalks.
4. Make a log pile to provide food and shelter for wood-eating beetle larvae.
5. Cut a hollow garden cane into short lengths and push them into a flowerpot on its side. Ladybugs will use it as a hibernation house during the winter.

a.

b.

c.

d.

e.

Which Is Which?

Scientists who study insects are called entomologists. Part of their work is to identify the many different kinds of insects and sort them into groups, and every year they discover thousands of new species. By studying insects, scientists learn more about how they live and how they affect us. This research can help us develop new ways of fighting disease and protecting crops.

Insect classification

This table gives details about the main orders (groups) of insects, but some facts are missing. Fill in the missing information using page 7 and the example species listed to help you.

Picture	Common name	Scientific name	Number of species	Key features	Example species
	....	Hymenoptera	....	Narrow waist; two pairs of wings; many species are armed with stings; often live in large colonies	Common wasp
	....	Coleoptera	....	Hard front wings fit over rear wings like a case	Stag beetle
	....	Hemiptera	....	Piercing or sucking mouthparts; most species have wings	Shield bug
	....	Lepidoptera	....	Covered in tiny scales; two pairs of broad wings; tubelike mouthparts	Monarch butterfly
	Caddisflies	Trichoptera	15,000	Larvae live in water and build a protective case from stones; adults are mothlike	Net-spinning caddisfly
	C..................	Blattodea	4,500	Chewing mouthparts; body is flat and oval	Hissing cockroach

Picture	Common name	Scientific name	Number of species	Key features	Example species
	....	Orthoptera	....	Strongly built body; powerful back legs; chewing mouthparts	Bush cricket
	....	Odonata	....	Adults have a long body, two pairs of long wings, and large eyes; larvae live in fresh water	Hawker dragonfly
	E......................	Dermaptera	2,000	Long, flat body that ends in a pair of pincers	Common earwig
	F......................	Siphonaptera	2,200	Wingless parasites that live on mammals and birds; blood-sucking mouthparts	Cat flea
	....	Diptera	....	Single pair of wings; large eyes; sucking or biting mouthparts	Robber fly
	Praying mantises	Mantodea	2,400	Long body; huge front legs armed with spines; very large eyes	Orchid mantis
	S......................	Zygentoma	560	Wingless, slender body, covered with silvery, fishlike scales	Common silverfish
	S...................... and leaf insects	Phasmatodea	3000	Slender body, usually camouflaged to look like leaves or twigs	Stick insect
	T......................	Isoptera	3,000	Live in large colonies; workers are wingless and have strong chewing mouthparts	Harvester termite

The First Insects

Insects were among the first animals to live on land. They appeared 400 million years ago, long before the dinosaurs, and probably were scavengers. The earliest winged insects took to the skies more than 300 million years ago. Insects survived the global climate change that killed off the dinosaurs 65 million years ago and evolved into one of the world's most successful animal groups.

Did you know?

Meganeura, a giant dragonfly-like species, was the largest known flying insect ever to have lived.

Meganeura had an enormous wingspan of 2.5 ft (75 cm).

Match the insect fossils

Fossilization is a process by which dead animals are slowly turned to stone, or leave other traces such as footprints, that remain preserved over millions of years. Look carefully at these fossils of five different ancient insects, then draw a line to match each fossil to the most similar insect alive today.

Insect fossils

a.   b.   c.   d.   e.

Insects today

1. Cranefly   2. Fly   3. Earwig   4. Dragonfly   5. Cockroach

Insect evolution

Read the following sentences about the evolution of insects. Then number the statements 1 to 4 to put them in the correct order of events, using the information on this page to help you.

Silverfish

Magnolia flower

a. Silverfish give us an idea of what the world's oldest insects might have been like.

b. The first flowers that bloomed on Earth provided food for several new types of insects, such as bees.

c. The ancestors of insects were tiny sea animals.

d. Dragonflies appeared about 300 million years ago.

Ancient insect facts

- Insects evolved from small sea creatures that crawled onto land 420 million years ago.

- The first insects evolved 400 million years ago and may have looked like today's wingless silverfish.

- Cockroaches and dragonflies emerged about 300 million years ago, when lush forests covered much of the Earth.

- Bees appeared soon after the first flowering plants, around 100 million years ago.

Studying Insects

Insects are all around us and affect our lives in many ways, so studying them is an important area of science. It can also be great fun. All you need to study insects are alert eyes and plenty of patience. A notebook, digital camera, and magnifying glass will come in useful, too.

Keep an insect diary

One of the best ways to study insects is to watch them and note what they do. You can record your findings on this chart.

1 Use the first two columns to record the date and location of each insect sighting you make.

2 Write down any interesting behavior in the next column— for example, if the insect was eating something.

3 Try to identify the insects you have seen using an insect guide or a website, and write their names in the last column.

Date	Location	Behavior	Name of insect

Bug hunting

Many bugs and other insects are good at hiding, but with the help of a tray, you can get a much closer look at them. The best time to hunt for insects is a warm summer day, when most species are active.

! Don't touch or pick up any insects you collect because they may bite or sting. After you've looked at them, allow them to crawl or fly away.

1 Cut a piece of white paper or card stock to line the bottom of your tray.

2 Put the tray under a bush, flower, or leafy branch. Then gently tap the plant or branch with a stick.

3 Carefully remove the tray to see what has tumbled out. Use a magnifying glass to get a close-up view of your insects. Try putting the tray in different places to see if you find any different insects, and note down what you collect.

4 Use this space to draw the most interesting insect you found.

Body Parts and Classifications

Check or number the boxes to answer each question. Check your answers on page 46.

1 How many legs do insects have?

- ☐ **a.** Four pairs
- ☐ **b.** Three pairs
- ☐ **c.** Two pairs
- ☐ **d.** It depends on the species

2 An insect's second body section is the:

- ☐ **a.** Wing
- ☐ **b.** Abdomen
- ☐ **c.** Thorax
- ☐ **d.** Leg

3 Select two animals that are *not* insects:

- ☐ **a.** Scorpion
- ☐ **b.** Silverfish
- ☐ **c.** Froghopper
- ☐ **d.** Spider

4 When did insects first appear on Earth?

- ☐ **a.** 400 million years ago
- ☐ **b.** 2 billion years ago
- ☐ **c.** 400,000 years ago
- ☐ **d.** 100 million years ago

5 A dragonfly's compound eyes contain thousands of:

- ☐ **a.** Mirrors
- ☐ **b.** Hairs
- ☐ **c.** Lenses
- ☐ **d.** Bones

6 What is the world's largest group of insects?

- ☐ **a.** Bugs
- ☐ **b.** Flies
- ☐ **c.** Butterflies and moths
- ☐ **d.** Beetles

7 What does a beetle use its mandibles for?

- ☐ **a.** Mating
- ☐ **b.** Feeding
- ☐ **c.** Flying
- ☐ **d.** Swimming

8 Select all the things insects use their antennae for:

- ☐ **a.** Smell
- ☐ **b.** Taste
- ☐ **c.** Finding mates
- ☐ **d.** Breathing

9 Which of these insects are the only ones covered in tiny scales?

- ☐ **a.** Butterflies and moths
- ☐ **b.** Ants
- ☐ **c.** Wasps
- ☐ **d.** Earwigs

10 A grasshopper's ears are on its:

- ☐ **a.** Head
- ☐ **b.** Legs
- ☐ **c.** Abdomen
- ☐ **d.** It doesn't have any

Habitats, Burrows, and Nests

Check or number the boxes to answer each question. Check your answers on page 46.

1 Which habitat has the most different kinds of insects?

- ☐ **a.** Desert
- ☐ **b.** Fields
- ☐ **c.** Rain forest
- ☐ **d.** Gardens

2 Where do diving beetles live?

- ☐ **a.** Caves
- ☐ **b.** Ponds
- ☐ **c.** In the soil
- ☐ **d.** On cliffs

3 What is the only place on Earth without any insects?

- ☐ **a.** High mountains
- ☐ **b.** The Antarctic
- ☐ **c.** Hot springs
- ☐ **d.** Deep sea

4 Which insect larvae burrow inside dead trees?

- ☐ **a.** Beetles
- ☐ **b.** Stick insects
- ☐ **c.** Fleas
- ☐ **d.** Mole crickets

5 The main reason butterflies and moths visit flowers is:

- ☐ **a.** To mate
- ☐ **b.** To rest
- ☐ **c.** To eat pollen
- ☐ **d.** To drink nectar

6 How many termites live in the largest termite mounds?

- ☐ **a.** 5,000
- ☐ **b.** 50,000
- ☐ **c.** 500,000
- ☐ **d.** 5,000,000

7 A family group of insects living together is called a:

- ☐ **a.** Band
- ☐ **b.** Species
- ☐ **c.** Herd
- ☐ **d.** Colony

8 Which of these insects is *not* a type of honeybee?

- ☐ **a.** Queen
- ☐ **b.** Worker
- ☐ **c.** Nymph
- ☐ **d.** Drone

9 Which insect digs a burrow for its larvae to live in?

- ☐ **a.** Thorn bug
- ☐ **b.** Dung beetle
- ☐ **c.** Bombardier beetle
- ☐ **d.** Shield bug

10 Number these steps 1 to 5 to show how a wasp nest develops:

- ☐ **a.** The queen lays eggs in the cells.
- ☐ **b.** The workers look after the nest.
- ☐ **c.** The larvae hatch into workers.
- ☐ **d.** The eggs hatch into larvae.
- ☐ **e.** The queen makes cells.

Reproduction and Life Cycle

Check or number the boxes to answer each question. Check your answers on page 46.

1 How do most insects breed?

- ☐ **a.** Swarming
- ☐ **b.** Sexual reproduction
- ☐ **c.** Cloning
- ☐ **d.** Asexual reproduction

2 Which insects give birth to live young?

- ☐ **a.** Beetles
- ☐ **b.** Wasps
- ☐ **c.** Aphids
- ☐ **d.** Flies

3 Stag beetles fight because they are:

- ☐ **a.** Young squabbling
- ☐ **b.** A male and female taking part in courtship
- ☐ **c.** Males wrestling for a chance to mate
- ☐ **d.** Females trying to impress watching males

4 Where does a caterpillar change into an adult butterfly or moth?

- ☐ **a.** In a nest
- ☐ **b.** In an egg
- ☐ **c.** In a pupa
- ☐ **d.** Underground

5 Cicadas are a type of bug that attract a mate by:

- ☐ **a.** Singing
- ☐ **b.** Fighting
- ☐ **c.** Dancing
- ☐ **d.** Scent

6 Which of these insects do *not* look after their young?

- ☐ **a.** Termites
- ☐ **b.** Dragonflies
- ☐ **c.** Earwigs
- ☐ **d.** Ants

7 How long does a housefly take to complete its entire life cycle?

- ☐ **a.** Six months
- ☐ **b.** Six weeks
- ☐ **c.** Six days
- ☐ **d.** Six hours

8 Which of these insects grow up by incomplete metamorphosis?

- ☐ **a.** Moths
- ☐ **b.** Wasps
- ☐ **c.** Bugs
- ☐ **d.** Bees

9 Select two ways that you can tell a baby cockroach from its parents:

- ☐ **a.** It lacks legs.
- ☐ **b.** It is wingless.
- ☐ **c.** It is a different color.
- ☐ **d.** It is smaller.

10 Number these steps 1 to 4 to describe the life cycle of a butterfly:

- ☐ **a.** Larva
- ☐ **b.** Adult
- ☐ **c.** Egg
- ☐ **d.** Pupa

Feeding and Defense

Check or number the boxes to answer each question. Check your answers on page 46.

1 What do red admiral caterpillars feed on?

- ☐ **a.** Vegetables
- ☐ **b.** Stinging nettles
- ☐ **c.** Roses
- ☐ **d.** Grass

2 Select two types of insects with sucking mouthparts:

- ☐ **a.** Housefly
- ☐ **b.** Goliath beetle
- ☐ **c.** Praying mantis
- ☐ **d.** Assassin bug

3 Butterflies and moths drink nectar using their:

- ☐ **a.** Stamen
- ☐ **b.** Thorax
- ☐ **c.** Proboscis
- ☐ **d.** Spiracles

4 Select three things eaten by insect scavengers:

- ☐ **a.** Dead bodies
- ☐ **b.** Pollen
- ☐ **c.** Rotting plants
- ☐ **d.** Leftover food

5 What enables the larva of a longhorn beetle to eat solid wood?

- ☐ **a.** Microorganisms in its gut
- ☐ **b.** Venom
- ☐ **c.** A chemical that dissolves wood
- ☐ **d.** Sticky saliva

6 How does the ant lion larva catch its prey?

- ☐ **a.** Hunts in packs
- ☐ **b.** Digs a trap
- ☐ **c.** Spins a web
- ☐ **d.** Uses its sting

7 Fleas are a type of:

- ☐ **a.** Herbivore
- ☐ **b.** Scavenger
- ☐ **c.** Predator
- ☐ **d.** Parasite

8 How does the weta defend itself?

- ☐ **a.** Runs for cover
- ☐ **b.** Rolls into a ball
- ☐ **c.** Digs itself a hole
- ☐ **d.** Waves its legs

9 Why do insect-eating birds leave hoverflies alone?

- ☐ **a.** They release a foul smell.
- ☐ **b.** They are poisonous.
- ☐ **c.** They look like wasps.
- ☐ **d.** They have sharp spines.

10 Why do some moths have colorful eyespots on their wings?

- ☐ **a.** To help them see
- ☐ **b.** To frighten predators
- ☐ **c.** To attract their prey
- ☐ **d.** To help them hide

Insects on the Move

Check or number the boxes to answer each question. Check your answers on page 46.

1 Which insects fly the fastest?

- ☐ **a.** Wasps
- ☐ **b.** Butterflies
- ☐ **c.** Hawkmoths
- ☐ **d.** Flies

2 Where are an insect's flight muscles?

- ☐ **a.** In its thorax
- ☐ **b.** In its abdomen
- ☐ **c.** In its wings
- ☐ **d.** Under its wings

3 Which of these insects has more than one pair of wings?

- ☐ **a.** Gnats
- ☐ **b.** Dragonflies
- ☐ **c.** Midges
- ☐ **d.** Mosquitoes

4 Which insects run the fastest?

- ☐ **a.** Fleas
- ☐ **b.** Ants
- ☐ **c.** Beetles
- ☐ **d.** Stick insects

5 Why doesn't a pond skater sink?

- ☐ **a.** It skates quickly.
- ☐ **b.** It weighs so little.
- ☐ **c.** It clings on with its claws.
- ☐ **d.** It hovers just above the surface.

6 Select two things that describe a beetle's rear wings:

- ☐ **a.** Thin
- ☐ **b.** Thick
- ☐ **c.** Transparent
- ☐ **d.** Heavy

7 Select two kinds of flying insects that are even older than the dinosaurs:

- ☐ **a.** Caddisflies
- ☐ **b.** Dragonflies
- ☐ **c.** Cockroaches
- ☐ **d.** Moths

8 How far can a locust jump?

- ☐ **a.** 20 in (50 cm)
- ☐ **b.** 33 ft (10 m)
- ☐ **c.** 7 ft (2 m)
- ☐ **d.** 2 in (5 cm)

9 Which insect spends its entire life upside down?

- ☐ **a.** Horsefly
- ☐ **b.** Woodworm
- ☐ **c.** Froghopper
- ☐ **d.** Water boatman

10 Why does a grasshopper rub its legs against its wings?

- ☐ **a.** To get ready to jump
- ☐ **b.** To make a buzzing song
- ☐ **c.** To take off
- ☐ **d.** To warm up on cold days

Insects and People

Check or number the boxes to answer each question. Check your answers on page 46.

1 Scientists who study insects are called:

- ☐ **a.** Geologists
- ☐ **b.** Entomologists
- ☐ **c.** Hydrologists
- ☐ **d.** Ornithologists

2 What is the name for the task of identifying species and sorting them into different groups?

- ☐ **a.** Organization
- ☐ **b.** Species sorting
- ☐ **c.** Fossilization
- ☐ **d.** Classification

3 How much of the world's crops do insects ruin each year?

- ☐ **a.** 15 percent
- ☐ **b.** 50 percent
- ☐ **c.** 5 percent
- ☐ **d.** 1 percent

4 Which of these insects is not a garden pest?

- ☐ **a.** Planthopper
- ☐ **b.** Mealy bug
- ☐ **c.** Ladybug
- ☐ **d.** Aphid

5 Number these steps 1 to 5 to show how malaria spreads in people:

- ☐ **a.** The parasite passes into the person's bloodstream.
- ☐ **b.** An infected mosquito bites someone.
- ☐ **c.** The parasite rapidly multiplies.
- ☐ **d.** The parasite invades the victim's liver.
- ☐ **e.** The victim suffers a high fever.

6 Select two insects that can cause havoc in kitchens and food stores:

- ☐ **a.** Mealworm
- ☐ **b.** Woodworm
- ☐ **c.** Stag beetle
- ☐ **d.** Larder beetle

7 Which of these things is not usually used for studying insects?

- ☐ **a.** Digital camera
- ☐ **b.** Telescope
- ☐ **c.** Magnifying glass
- ☐ **d.** Kitchen tray

8 Select two useful things that honeybees do:

- ☐ **a.** They make silk.
- ☐ **b.** They produce beeswax.
- ☐ **c.** They pollinate crops.
- ☐ **d.** They control pests.

9 What is the main threat to dragonflies?

- ☐ **a.** Cutting down trees
- ☐ **b.** Hunting
- ☐ **c.** Wetland drainage
- ☐ **d.** Road building

10 Wild bees are threatened by:

- ☐ **a.** Using too much weed killer
- ☐ **b.** Burning leaves
- ☐ **c.** Tourism
- ☐ **d.** Modern building techniques

Activity Answers

Once you have completed each page of activities, check your answers below.

Page 14
The parts of a beetle
1. antenna
2. mandible
3. head
4. thorax
5. front leg
6. wing case
7. middle leg
8. wing
9. abdomen
10. rear leg

Insect look-alikes
1. **moth**—insect
2. **centipede**—not an insect
3. **spider**—not an insect
4. **weevil**—insect
5. **fly**—insect

Page 15
Wasp alert!
... uses its pair of **antennae** ...
... a massive **compound eye** ...
... thousands of tiny **lenses** ...
... there are three **simple eyes** ...
... covered with sensitive **hairs** ...

Feeling around
1. e 2. d 3. a 4. b 5. c

Page 16
Lift-off!

Page 16
Mix-and-match legs
1. d 2. a 3. c 4. e 5. b

Page 17
Different diets quiz
1. chewing
2. predators
3. needlelike
4. dead animals
5. parasites
6. plant-sucking

Food web puzzle
1. c 2. d 3. b 4. e 5. a

Page 18
Young insects puzzle
1. damselfly nymph
2. cockroach nymph
3. bug nymph
4. froghopper nymph

Insect metamorphosis
Beetles—complete
Grasshoppers and crickets—incomplete
Butterflies and moths—complete
Dragonflies and damselflies—incomplete
Flies—complete
Ants, bees, and wasps—complete
Bugs—incomplete
Cockroaches—incomplete

Page 20
Insect predator quiz
1. assassin bug
2. great diving beetle
3. front legs
4. in groups
5. its sting
6. ladybug

Page 20
Wasp sting
... at the end of its **abdomen** ...
... The sharp **barb** at the tip ...
... in the wasp's **venom sac** ...
...A powerful **muscular pouch** pumps the venom ...

Page 21
Hide and seek puzzle
1. d 2. a 3. e 4. c 5. b

Avoiding predators
a. 5 b. 1 c. 4 d. 2 e. 3

Page 22
Insect habitats
Rain forest—giant Atlas moth
Cave—cave crickets
Grassland—Dung beetles
Desert—desert beetles
Stream—Dragonflies
Garden—bumblebees

Page 23
True or false?
1. True
2. False—When an insect hibernates, its body processes slow down.
3. False—Muddy ponds have enough oxygen for fly larvae to live there.
4. True
5. False—Several kinds of insects can live on high mountains.

Survival strategies
1. external
2. temperature
3. air
4. less
5. a single entrance hole

Page 24
True or false?
1. False—Only the colony's queen honeybee lays eggs.
2. True
3. True

4. False—Worker honeybees are always female.
5. True

Termite city
1. ventilation chimney
2. side vents
3. nursery chambers
4. royal cell
5. clay wall

Page 25
Building a nest
1. d 2. f 3. c 4. a 5. e 6. b

Together or alone?
1. ant—lives together
2. grasshopper—lives alone
3. honeybee—lives together
4. termite—lives together
5. mantis—lives alone

Page 26
Identification puzzle
... some of the most **eye-catching** ...
... moths tend to be **dull and drab** ...
... at night or **during the day** ...
... butterflies never fly **after dark** ...
... Moths have **thicker** antennae ...
... normally holds its wings **flat** ...
... likely to keep its wings **folded**.

Page 27
Bluebottle life span
Egg—24 hours
Maggot—10 days
Pupa—12 days
Adult—2–3 weeks
Total life span—6 weeks

Population explosion
There will now be 2,000,000 flies, because the 10,000 breeding couples each produced 200 young (10,000 x 200 = 2,000,000).

Mopping up
1. liquid
2. saliva

3. dissolve the food
4. spongelike

Page 28
Fighting beetles
1. females
2. jaws
3. antennae
4. lift up
5. loser

Page 28
Beetling about
1. **ladybug larva**—aphid
2. **violin beetle**—snail
3. **mealworm**—flour
4. **goliath beetle**—fruit
5. **fungus weevil**—mushrooms

Page 29
Walking on water
The paper clip floats on the water. This is because water has a thin surface "skin." Like a pond skater, the paper clip is very light, so it can rest on the water's skin without sinking. Heavier objects, such as coins, are too heavy for the water surface to support, which is why they fall through and sink to the bottom. Try it and see!

Mealtime
1. **planthopper**—vegetarian
2. **pond skater**—predator
3. **assassin bug**—predator
4. **mealy bug**—vegetarian
5. **sea skater**—predator

True or false?
1. False—Some bugs, including several kinds of assassin bugs, can spread disease when they bite humans.
2. True
3. False—Mealy bugs are tiny. The world's largest bugs are giant water bugs.

4. True
5. True

Page 30
Nature's helpers
1. scavenge
2. pollinate
3. spin
4. control
5. crush

Page 30
Made by insects
1. Silk scarves are made from silk produced by **silkworms**.
2. Some candles are made from beeswax, produced by **honeybees**.
3. Cochineal food coloring is made from the crushed bodies of **scale insects**.
4. Honey is made by **honeybees**.

Page 31
Pollination puzzle
Perfumed **petals** attract insects
Antennae detect flower's scent
Proboscis sucks up flower nectar
Long **stamens** hold flower pollen
Hairy body dusted with pollen grains

Cleaning up
The dung beetle gathers bits of cattle dung and pats them into a **ball**. This is usually **larger** than the beetle itself. It uses its strong **legs** to push the dung along the ground. Next, the beetle digs a **tunnel** as a nest. It fills the nest with plenty of dung for its **grubs** to eat. Finally, the beetle lays its eggs and seals the entrance to the nest.

Page 32
True or false?
1. True
2. False—Malaria does kill millions of people every year, but most people infected with it survive.
3. True
4. True

5. False—Malaria parasites reproduce inside the infected person's liver.

Insect damage
1. woodworm
2. clothes moth
3. caterpillar
4. larder beetle

Page 33
Insect threat test
1. beetles
2. wasps and ants
3. beetles and butterflies
4. dragonflies
5. bees

Create an insect refuge
1. e 2. a 3. b 4. d 5. c

Pages 34–35
Insect classification
Ants, bees, and wasps—
  150,000 species
Beetles—400,000 species
Bugs—103,000 species
Butterflies and moths—
  180,000 species
Cockroaches
Crickets and grasshoppers—
  25,000 species
Dragonflies and damselflies—
  6,000 species

Earwigs
Fleas
Flies—160,000 species
Silverfish
Stick and leaf insects
Termites

Page 36
Match the insect fossils
1. c 2. e 3. b 4. a 5. d

Insect evolution
a. 3 b. 1 c. 4 d. 2

Quick Quiz Answers

Once you have completed each page of quiz questions, check your answers below.

Page 38
1. b 2. c 3. a, d 4. a 5. c 6. d 7. b
8. a, b, c 9. a 10. c

Page 39
1. c 2. b 3. d 4. a 5. d 6. d 7. d
8. c 9. b 10. a 2, b 5, c 4, d 3, e 1

Page 40
1. b 2. c 3. c 4. c 5. a 6. b 7. b

8. c 9. b, d 10. a 2, b 4, c 1, d 3

Page 41
1. b 2. a, d 3. c 4. a, c, d 5. a 6. b
7. d 8. d 9. c 10. b

Page 42
1. c 2. a 3. b 4. c 5. b 6. a, c
7. b, c 8. c 9. d 10. b

Page 43
1. b 2. d 3. a 4. c
5. a 2, b 1, c 4, d 3, e 5
6. a, d 7. b 8. b, c 9. c 10. a

Acknowledgments

The publisher would like to thank the following:

Julie Ferris for proofreading, Derek Harvey for 2020 consultant review, and Harish Aggarwal, and Priyanka Sharma for the jacket

The publisher would like to thank the following for their kind permission to reproduce their photographs:

(Key: a-above; b-below/bottom; c-center; f-far; l-left; r-right; t-top)

DK Images: 6 Jerry Young (cla). 7 Jerry Young (fcra -wood louse). 9 Natural History Museum, London (cra). 10 Natural History Museum, London (cl). 12 Natural History Museum, London (tr); Oxford Scientific Films (bl); Natural History Museum, London (tr). 14 Natural History Museum, London (cr). 15 Natural History Museum, London (br -insect b). 16 Natural History Museum, London (bc). 18 Natural History Museum, London (cra) (br) (cr) (cra). 21 Natural History Museum, London (bl); Jerry Young (cla -insect 1). 26 Booth Museum of Natural History, Brighton (tr). 28 Natural History Museum, London (bl). 30 Stephen Oliver (bl). 31 Natural History Museum, London, EMU Unit (fcra).

34 Natural History Museum, London (clb); Jerry Young (cla) (c -earwig) (ca -insect fossil c) (cl -fly) (cla -insect fossil b) (cr -dragonfly). 36 Natural History Museum, London (fcrb); Oxford University Museum of Natural History (fcra -insect fossil e); Lindsey Stock (bl). 42 James Kuether (cb).**Dreamstime.com:** 28 Rudmer Zwerver (clb -snail eating beetle).

All other images © Dorling Kindersley
For further information see:
www.dkimages.com

INSECT RECORDS

RECORD	LONGEST INSECT	HEAVIEST INSECT	SMALLEST INSECT
NAME	Borneo stick insect	African Goliath beetle	Fairyfly
DETAILS	Max length 14 in (36 cm)	Max weight 3.4 oz (100 g)	0.006 in (0.017 cm) long
HABITAT	Rain forest	Rain forest	Inside other insects' eggs
DIET	Leaves	Tree sap, fruit	Insect eggs

RECORD	FASTEST RUNNER	LONGEST-LIVED INSECT	HIGHEST JUMPER
NAME	Tiger beetle	Periodical cicada	Froghopper
DETAILS	Top speed 3 ft/sec (1 m/sec)	17-year life cycle	Jumps over 2 ft (60 cm)
HABITAT	Warm sandy areas	Larva lives underground	Vegetation worldwide
DIET	Other insects	Larva eats plant roots	Plant juices

RECORD	LARGEST SWARM	FASTEST WINGBEATS	MOST DANGEROUS INSECT
NAME	Desert locust	Midge	Mosquito
DETAILS	Up to 40 billion locusts per swarm	Wings beat 50,000 times a minute	Spreads deadly malaria
HABITAT	Farmland in Africa and Asia	Near fresh water	Warm climates worldwide
DIET	Crops	Blood, Nectar	Blood, Nectar

RECORD	BEST SENSE OF SMELL	LOUDEST INSECT	BIGGEST APPETITE
NAME	Indian moon moth	African cicada	Polyphemus moth caterpillar
DETAILS	Smells a mate 7 miles (11 km) away	Song reaches 106 decibels	Eats 86,000 times its own weight in two months
HABITAT	Tropical Asia	Woodland	Woodland, orchards
DIET	Caterpillar eats leaves	Larva eats plant juices	Leaves of trees

INSECT PREDATORS

PREDATOR	7-SPOT LADYBUG	FLOWER MANTIS	TWINSPOT ASSASSIN BUG
PREY	APHIDS	BUTTERFLIES, BEES	OTHER INSECTS
KILL METHOD	POWERFUL JAWS	STRIKES WITH FRONT LEGS	INJECTS POISONOUS SALIVA
SIZE	$\frac{1}{3}$ IN (8 MM)	UP TO 3 IN (8 CM)	$1\frac{1}{2}$ IN (4 CM)
HABITAT	GARDENS AND FIELDS	INSIDE FLOWERS	TROPICAL VEGETATION

PREDATOR	WEEVIL WASP	WOOD ANT	GREAT DIVING BEETLE LARVA
PREY	WEEVILS	ANY SMALL PREY	INSECTS, TADPOLES, FISH
KILL METHOD	VENOMOUS STING	HUNTS IN GROUPS	POWERFUL JAWS
SIZE	$\frac{3}{4}$ IN (2 CM)	$\frac{3}{8}$ IN (1 CM)	UP TO $2\frac{1}{2}$ IN (6 CM)
HABITAT	SANDY AREAS	WOODLAND	PONDS

PREDATOR	TARANTULA HAWK (A WASP)	EMPEROR DRAGONFLY	WATER SCORPION
PREY	TARANTULAS	FLIES, MIDGES, GNATS	INSECTS, FISH
KILL METHOD	VENOMOUS STING	GRABS PREY IN MIDAIR	PINCERLIKE FRONT LEGS
SIZE	UP TO $2\frac{3}{4}$ IN (7 CM)	3 IN (8 CM)	$\frac{3}{4}$ IN (2 CM)
HABITAT	DESERT	PONDS, STREAMS	PONDS

PREDATOR	SNAIL-EATING BEETLE	ROBBER FLY	HAIRY ROVE BEETLE
PREY	SNAILS	OTHER INSECTS	BEETLE LARVAE, MAGGOTS
KILL METHOD	BITES WITH LONG JAWS	INJECTS POISONOUS SALIVA	STRONG JAWS
SIZE	$\frac{4}{5}$ IN (2 CM)	UP TO $\frac{2}{3}$ IN (1.5 CM)	$\frac{3}{4}$ IN (2 CM)
HABITAT	WOODLAND	GRASSLAND	ANIMAL DUNG